From Earthen Vessels

Copyright: © 2007 Compiled by Pamela Mae Rhew Bush
All Rights Reserved

Copyright: © 2007 Joanne Tolles
Copyright: © 2007 Joan C Dyer
Copyright: © 2007 Sandy Nettles
Copyright: © 2007 Shelly Cephas
Copyright: © 2007 Gail McNeill
Copyright: © 2007 Janice M. Pickett
Copyright: © 2007 Valerie Pererson Brown
Copyright: © 2007 Joyce Josephson
Copyright: © 2007 Marianna Yenenitzi
Copyright: © 2007 Melissa Sanders
Copyright: © 2007 Carla Procida
Copyright: © 2007 Bob Barra
Copyright: © 2007 Debi Kinch
Copyright: © 2007 Vickie Mosely
Copyright: © 2007 Diane L. Busch
Copyright: © 2007 Pamela Mae Rhew Bush
Copyright: © 2007 Frank Hanson

The copyright is held by each individual poet for their own work.
All Rights Reserved

IBSN 978-0-6151-7106-7

This book of poetry is
dedicated
to
God the Father, God the Son
and
God the Holy Spirit.

Acknowledgements

In compiling this collection of work, I would like to thank Kevin Watts, the founder of AllPoetry.com. This website has provided an avenue and opportunity for poets to network and share their work.

I would also like to thank the poem contributors. They come from all over the world, with various backgrounds and experiences. Their common link is their personal relationship with Jesus Christ.

Special thanks to Melissa Sanders for the cover sketching.

A big thank you to Vickie Mosely for helping out with some editing of bio's and helping to write the acknowledgements as well as the back cover. You are always there for me, and I appreciate you.

This collection would not have been possible if not for the life changing love and power of our Lord Jesus Christ.

Table of Contents

Page
- **11**............................**Joanne Tolles**
- 12................................ Biography
- 13................................Kiss the Sun
- 14................................Send Your Fire
- 15................................Torn and Tattered
- 16................................Forever and a Day
- 17................................Autumn Psalm
- **19**............................**Joan C. Dyer**
- 20................................Biography
- 21................................His Loving Peace
- 22................................Hand In Hand
- 23................................Guiding Footsteps
- 24................................Peaceful Calmness
- 25................................God's Finale'
- **27**............................**Sandy Nettles**
- 28................................Biography
- 29................................Along The Path
- 30................................Worship at Sunset
- 31................................Use Me Lord
- 32................................Redeemed
- 33................................Weary Child
- **35**............................**Shelly Cephas**
- 36................................Biography
- 37................................You Can Trust Him
- 38................................Back in the Fold
- 39................................Sunshine
- 40................................In His Grace We Work
- 41................................Our Savior
- **43**............................**Gail McNeill**
- 44................................Biography
- 45................................In The Wings
- 46................................Ocean Rain
- 47................................Forgiveness is Key
- 48................................Follow Me
- 49................................Second Chances

51	**Janice M. Pickett**
52	Biography
53	The Gift of Spirit
54	Heaven in My Sight
55	The Enemy EGO
56	Blessings
57	Heavenly Messenger
59	**Valerie Peterson Brown**
60	Biography
61	Our Lighthouse
62	The Person I Want To Be
63	Be With Me Lord I Pray
64	My Prayer
65	The Love of the Father
67	**Joyce Josephson**
68	Biography
69	Love
70	Hand of Grace
71	The Cornerstone
72	His Peace Will Reign
73	Feed the Need
75	**Marianna Yenenitzi**
76	Biography
77	Glorious Love and Adoration
78	Rejoice My Heart, My Soul, My Mind
79	God's Powerful Call
80	The Redeeming Hand of God
81	The Quiet Place Up High
83	**Melissa Sanders**
84	Biography
85	In His Peace
86	Passing All Understanding
87	Errant Faith
88	Cleansing Rain
89	Let Me Be Found

91	**Carla Procida**
92	Biography
93	All Our Dark Clouds
94	A Friend That Sticks Close
95	Taking God's Word to the Heights
96	Drops Beautifying
97	A Perfect Side
99	**Bob Barra**
100	Biography
101	About Faith
102	The Highest Form
103	Plea
104	Eternal Joy
105	Power of Three
107	**Debi Kinch**
108	Biography
109	Free to Whoever Wants
110	Thank You
111	In You
112	Nowhere to Hide
113	My King
115	**Vickie Mosely**
116	Biography
117	God Places Value
118	False Witness
119	Promise
120	Have I Thanked You
121	Remaking Me
123	**Diane L. Busch**
124	Biography
125	My Hurt
126	Lord
127	Graven Upon the Palms of His Hands
128	Praise
129	Weak Things

131...................................**Pamela Mae Rhew Bush**
132..................................Biography
133..................................Happiness Overflows
134..................................My Father
135..................................You Hold My Happiness
136..................................Always There
137..................................I Thank You God
139..................................**Frank Hanson**
141..................................Biography
142..................................True Balance
143..................................My Prayer
144..................................I Will Follow
145..................................Lord, Who Will I Be
Closing by Frank Hanson and Pamela Mae Rhew Bush
146..................................A Moment With The Lord
147..................................Altar Call

~~~~~~~~~~~~~~~~~~~~~~~~~~~~~
JoanneTolles
New Fairfield, Connecticut
~~~~~~~~~~~~~~~~~~~~~~~~~~~~~

Joanne Tolles is an English teacher at a small Alternative High School in CT. She loves to write, read, garden, SCUBA dive, and breed pure breed Golden Retrievers. She lives with her precious husband Bill and two golden dogs Chowder and Autumn and new kitten Gracie. She has two grown stepchildren and one wonderful grandson, who is the apple of her eye and her hope for tomorrow. She is a born-again Christian and ex-alcoholic. She was introduced to AllPoetry.com by one of her students in 2005 and uses AP when teaching poetry. She is a Teacher/Writing Consultant for the Connecticut Writing Project at Fairfield University and holds a Master degree in Teaching from Cornell University. Writing is Joanne's obsession and teaching writing is her passion.

Kiss the Son

What is a holy kiss
pure and without sin or taint of sin
an embrace of highest magnitude
given in unselfish love?

Today my Lord whispers to me
to come to Him and be with Him
and love Him forever

Who has ever heard of
such an invitation of immense proportions?
such an incredible idea?
such a pure desire?

To offer a holy kiss
to my Savior
without sin
without lust
without unholy desire?

There will come a time
when this body is dust
and my thoughts are unremembered
and even my poetry and rhyme
will fade like Lothlorien
and be no more

Then my Lord and Savior will say to me
"Come my child, and sit awhile with Me
and see the grandeur that is
set before us here in eternity
come my child"

I will run to Him
and embrace Him
and I will
kiss the Son

Send Your Fire

Send Your holy fire
to flare up the ashen embers
in my soul

Send Your healing oil
to sooth the gashes
in my heart

Send Your fiercest wind
to stir up the gifting's
hidden under my stubbornness

Send Your cleansing rain
to saturate
my hardened thoughts

Only You can inspire me
only You can heal me
only You can chase out the foolishness
only You can revive me

once again

Torn and Tattered

Vast distances we've traveled from
worm to butterfly we've become
surviving nature's rage we flee
torn and tattered but still lovely

Hunted daily by predators
our battles go from shore to shore
never captured, we remain free
torn and tattered but still lovely

One last time we drink life's nectar
never again to feel a scar
we fly to heaven hopefully
torn and tattered but still lovely

Forever and a Day

From the depths of my darkness
I call out to you - my hope - my reason to live

From under my heavy blanket of fear
I reach for you - your help - your hand to hold

When I think I am breathing my last breath
I touch you - my life - my source of being

I give my life to you and seek your face
for you alone are my sweet spring of salvation

For you are my only answer - my reason - my mission
without your spotlight of love, I melt into blackness and am voided

How can I repay the great debt I owe you?
How can I tell you I love you so dearly?

I fall to my knees in your wondrous halo of love
and I sing praises only to you - forever and a day

Autumn Psalm

Oh death, where is your sting?
oh grave, where is your victory?
oh heavens, how can you not exalt the King?
oh my soul, how can you not praise the Lord?

As autumn creeps slowly towards wintertime
I stop and savor the scent of sweet decay
that lingers in the evening air
and can be seen in every browning leaf

While my neighbors decry the injustices of the day
and fret about the coming icy season
my own breath becomes a song of silent profession
of my love and devotion to a risen Lord

For my Lord and Savior has conquered death
my Master has closed the graveyard to my entrance
the heavens cry tears of joyous jubilation
while my soul sings sweet hymns to Jesus

Joan C. Dyer
Middle Grove, New York

Joan Dyer was born and has lived in upstate New York all her life. She is an avid reader and writer. Being a very spiratual person, she has written and self-published her book of prayer/poems called "Gathering Inspiration" which has garnered great satisfaction for her.

Joan has also written and published a number of children's stories, a book of poems, and an anthology of short, essay-type stories.

As she matures, both in age and in knowledge, Joan's lifelong dream of becoming a writer are slowly emerging. Her best quote is: "One can only hope for infamy, but it is a goal we must strive for always."

His Loving Peace

Close your eyes in worship
fold your hands in prayer
lift your joyous voices high
He is waiting for you there

He will fill your heart with gladness
while He watches from above
and even if you question it
you'll be smiled on with love

No one is exempt from knowing
all that peace can bring
just reach up, touch His hand
let your heart begin to sing

Hand In Hand

Marching ever forward
over mountainside and sand
His love will always guide us
as we journey hand in hand

Singing joyful praises
with every step we take
this is never something
our Good Lord will forsake

He will march along beside us
listening to our prayer
as He leads us straight to Glory
never stopping till we're there

Guiding Footsteps

The footsteps that I walk in
are much larger than my own
but those firm shapes, I will follow
along the road He's shown

I know that He will guide me
with each step along the way
for however long it takes us
a month, a year, a day

Aware that I have stumbled
I kneel and bow my head
then pray and ask forgiveness
as I feel his love instead

He leads me on that loresome road
there will be no turning back
and at the end He'll greet me
knowing I was right on track

Peaceful Calmness

Opening the door, I step outside
and look up above to the skies
stars twinkle, in luminous beauty
reflecting the light from my eyes

I kneel on God's grass in the darkness
and pray thankfully for this sight
for here, in His peaceful calmness
I know all is perfectly right

God's Finale'

Sunday, that special day of the week
when the voices in church abound
singing hymns of beautiful music
hoping He will hear the great sound

Louder and louder the voices
singing praises to God on high
we always know that He has heard
for they come back as echos that sigh

Finally, as a finale'
bright dancing angels He sends
to bless everyone, all the faithful
as He smiles and whispers "AMEN"

~~~~~~~~~~~~~~~~~~~~~~~~~~~~
Sandy Nettles
Pensacola, Florida
~~~~~~~~~~~~~~~~~~~~~~~~~~~~

Sandy Nettles is a simple southern gal who lives in Florida with her husband, son and dogs. She enjoys spending time with her grandchildren and pouring her heart out with pen and paper. She loves the Lord and likes to glorify him through poetry. Sandy is 44 years young.

Along The Path

Along the path you have carried me
one set of footprints upon the sand
you offered me hope through salvation
I'll be with you in the promised land

You saved my soul from the evil one
I'm no longer deceived by his ways
your loving arms my sanctuary
I worship thee oh Ancient of Days

You are a Lamp unto my feet Lord
no longer in darkness do I roam
for I journey in light beside thee
in the end heaven will be my home

I thank you for changing my life
with the prospect of eternity
I fear not what tomorrow will bring
along the path you will carry me

Worship at Sunset

The sun fades over the horizon
on yet another glorious day
I stand in awe of his majesty
raise my hands to the heavens and pray

Thank you Father for your creation
and the blessings you shower on me
I know this magnificent sunset
is but a glimpse of eternity

I bow my head in reverence now
to the creator of all I love
let your will be done here on the earth
as it is in the heaven's above

End my day on a positive note
as I worship the ancient of days
so long as I live but in the flesh
may I walk in the light of your ways

Use Me Lord

I humbly bow before you now
Heavenly Father hear my plea
there are many lost souls out there
who know not of eternity

My prayer is that you'll use me Lord
to plant a seed in someone's heart
that they might walk away from sin
and look to you for a fresh start

Help me provide an example
of what agape' love can do
when sinners get on bended knee
and open up there hearts to you

I long to lead someone to Christ
for salvation is their's to gain
once their life is given to you
true redemption will always reign

Use me as you see fit my Lord
for above all I do believe
the healing power of the cross
is still there for all to receive

Redeemed

I remember my wandering
yes, the bitterness and the gall
as I roamed about in darkness
when once I stumbled and did fall

Down to the abyss I spiraled
I could not see the light of day
thus heading straight for hell I was
with nothing standing in my way

Then someone took the time one day
shared with me of the Lord above
no longer did I need to live
in my lost world of push and shove

She told me about Jesus Christ
how he died on the cross for me
and told me that belief in him
would bring life in eternity

Got on my knees and bowed my head
begun to pray the sinners prayer
it became apparent to me
that I'd been saved right then and there

So now when the devil tempts me
I simply bow my head and pray
for when you call upon His name
the evil one will run away

Weary Child

Come take my hand weary child of mine
let me pull you from the mud and mire
fear not what earthly life has in store
for I alone shall be your desire

I'll wipe away your heartache and pain
as I plant your feet on solid ground
I will replace your sadness with joy
and I shall give you a mind that is sound

Straighten the narrow path before you
removing obstacles from your way
I'll walk in the darkness beside you
into the light of a brand new day

So take my hand weary child of mine
and let your life thus begin anew
for there's nothing more precious to me
than to spend eternity with you

~~~~~~~~~~~~~~~~~~~~~~~~~~~
Shelley Cephas
Brooklyn, New York
~~~~~~~~~~~~~~~~~~~~~~~~~~~

Shelley Cephas is a trained librarian who loves reading and writing poetry. A born again Christian, she was raised in Connecticut and moved to New York to attend graduate school at Pratt Institute. Upon graduation she made Brooklyn her home where she continues in her favorite pastime writing poetry. She has worked in corporate American for more than fifteen year as a documentation specialist. Presently she works in a university in New York.

You Can Trust Him

He is always with you wherever you go
to guide and protect you as you'll come to know
no trouble too difficult, He can't set right
just trust in His power, in Him you delight

His presence around you is sent from above
and wraps firmly about you, His gift of love
then reach out to Him, no matter where you are
there is no hiding from Him, no place too far

So take the chance and try calling out to Him
there's no need to fear because all of us sin
a friend always caring when others do not
in Him we can trust with whatever our lot

He laid down His life so we'd be forgiven
one day we'll join Him forever in heaven

Back in the Fold

When trouble starts to rear its ugly head
and shadows of the time are wrought for none
while friends begin to wonder what was said
to cause your hopes and dreams to come undone

This darkness seems to fill each coming day
no matter where you search for calm relief
and as you watch the path that leads the way
you tend to lose what's left of your belief

In desperation you call out to Him
and hope that He is listening today
because your problems have become so grim
to trust in Him is now your only way

The prodigal is welcomed in the fold
and now will receive gifts from Him untold

Sun Shine

The sun shines down upon the good and bad
a light to nurture life within its sight
and rises when you're happy or you're sad
its beauty should be treasured with delight

For God has blessed us with a lovely day
to soothe our souls of sorrow without cost
and as we walk through troubles in our way
it sometimes feels as though we must be lost

So gaze upon the beauty that you see
drink in its warmth to calm your distraught heart
in nature you will find that you can be
reborn so you can make a brand new start

Stand in the sunshine as it showers you
and joy within your heart God will renew

In His Grace We Work

Shall we at close of day put chores aside
and give our thanks to God for all He's done
it's in His love and grace that we abide
He gives us strength to make our daily run

Our work may not be all that we desire
although through it we manage to partake
and dream of days when from it we retire
to do those things we love for our Lord's sake

So find in life your happiness and joy
in Him who gives you hope to carry on
as you work diligently to enjoy
a new beginning that each day will dawn

Praise God for all the blessings He bestows
upon your life in grace you will repose

Our Savior

He came to earth to save the lost
and knew His life would be the cost
this is the reason He's adored
God's greatest gift, our precious Lord

In Him there is no taint of sin
and by Him we are gathered in
it's through Him that we are restored
God's greatest gift, our precious Lord

He gives us all His loving care
for His love is beyond compare
you'll find in Him your just reward
God's greatest gift, our precious Lord

He came to earth to save the lost
God's greatest gift, our precious Lord

~~~~~~~~~~~~~~~~~~~~~~~~~~
Gail McNeill
Anglesey, North Wales
~~~~~~~~~~~~~~~~~~~~~~~~~~

Gail McNeill writes under the pseudonym bethan-gaze (www.allpoetry.com/bethan-gaze). She has always found solace in the written word and has written extensively since the age of eleven. She has a degree in English and Writing and later trained to be a teacher with a placement at Styal Women's Prison. It was here that the Lord really impressed upon her the desire to seek His face and to witness for Him. She prayed with a number of girls in the Prison and when one of them became a Christian, she sensed that the Lord was calling her to Bible College. She is currently studying for an MA in Theology alongside her work as a Representative for the Suffering Church, and as an Advocate for Compassion. Gail lives in Anglesey with her husband and their four children.

In The Wings

Paradise comes in
the most unlikely places
there are glimpses of
new life emerging within
the furrows of barren soil

roused by the warmth of
the early morning sun that
breathes vitality
birthing opportunities
to shine in the darkest night

Wherever we are
you are there, also, in the
wings cheering us on
your gentle touch, a soft wind
a transparent butterfly

Ocean Rain

Looking out to sea, vessels on their way
to Ireland; huge cargo ships like thick-set
jowls on a slack jaw line
sometimes, half-raters take the journey
round the coast, their feeble sails
no match for the Anglesey wind
their pocket handkerchief colours dipping
precariously in aqua waters

Ocean rain at its best, cascading like
a rainy day in freefall. Such velocity is
captivating. I am spellbound by its
beauty, the way it mesmerizes with its
moods, chastises with its lack of candour
(the reflections of a thousand women)
whilst underneath, something more resilient
is in control

Something unseen. Then, my thoughts take in
the rocks, the boundaries allowing the
venting of emotion, the spilling out of
expression, like a vortex. Until it stops
and listens. And suddenly, it hits me - the
realisation, that all you ever wanted for me
is within my grasp ... when I choose to pause
for breath and give you control of my life

Forgiveness is Key

Mistakes are made, it's true to say
and hearts are broken in this way
but surely, true love conquers all
if we stumble, or if we fall
for no-one knows the road ahead
from the vows we make when we wed

We cannot change the things we've done
just learn from them, like anyone
can't you see forgiveness is key?
I forgive you, please forgive me

Follow Me

Sometimes, I catch a
glimpse of you in the shadows
a momentary
reminder of your presence
in the incandescent light

Your eyes penetrate
my negligent endeavour
to seek your beauty -
a reminder of the fact
that you are all around me

And I am humbled
who is doing the stalking?
I thought it was me
but my heart follows you ... such
beauty in your crown of thorns

Second Chances

The past is a void
laden with mistakes that lie
in a crevice of my heart
now labelled "no fishing"
yet, sometimes, in low
dry seasons, my mind meanders
over this rocky terrain to
mourn. Futility beckons
as she has always done

enticing me, reminding me
of my fall. If I listen, she
convinces me that hope
is lost, that doors are
closed, that defeat lies close
by ready to lick my wounds
it is only through tears
you hear the longing of my
heart. In the quietness, I

sense your presence, you
lift me with the varying hues of
seasonal days, the purity of
new birth, the promise of love
that we use glibly in kartwheel
shapes when we sign
letters. You show me your
seal, how it encompasses me
the fine letters that spell out
"forgiven"

~~~~~~~~~~~~~~~~~~~~~~~~~~~~
Janice M Pickett
Queensland Australia
~~~~~~~~~~~~~~~~~~~~~~~~~~~~

Janice M Pickett gave her heart to the Lord 25 years ago after suffering too many unhappy disasters for which she had no answers.
Her life did a complete turn around. From then on blessings flowed and her life became a spiritual pleasure, filled with a clear understanding of his presence in her life.

The Gift of Spirit

I have learned how to fly, reached the peak
touched the sky
skinned my knees, known the pain
but above all this, one thing I gained
I found my spirit, my reason to be
wrapped up as a gift from God to me
now I hold it close every day
it belongs to me in every way
it cannot be stolen, it cannot leave
it's a priceless gift, the best to receive
when I opened the package it flew into my soul
that spiritual gift that has made me whole

Heaven in My Sight

My Eyes opening
now I see
depth of vision increased
mind expanding
heart overflowing
spirit soaring
touched beyond belief
I am now whole

The Enemy EGO

Caress each day as if it were your very soul
drink in love as if it were water
soak up compassion as if you were a sponge
walk with open arms to welcome everyone
take nothing said to you in anger as a personal insult
smile in the face of verbal attack
look into your spirit and meditate
see the spirits around you with lessons on love
Be calm
Be real
Be one of the special group
who treasure life
who work for peace
who sow the seeds to heaven on earth
but mostly
BE TRUE TO THE HEART WITHIN YOU
there you will see the gentle soul
who has so much love to give
let that person come out
let them guide you daily
let each man woman and child
know the gentle touch from your spirit
if all men took the lead
then there would be no room for war

Blessings

Life now is more spiritual
spiritual and fulfilled
sharing spiritual blessings
as spiritual blessings are good

I want to be more spiritual
sprititual in my ways
spiritual in my actions
more spiritual all my days

I think to be so spiritual
you need a spiritual heart
a spiritual understanding
so your spiritual life can start

Heavenly Messenger

We hear them talk of angels wings
white and pure they be
but when I hear a strange telephone call
a pure white dove I see
for was it not that perfect dove
that flew out from the ark?
we found a new beginning and
came back from the dark
then in every Christian Movie
a vision can be seen
a dove flying past a camera
with light on wings that gleam
I will always think of the precious Dove
as a gift from way up high
a messenger that brings us love
as it passes by
so if I ever get the chance
to come back as a bird
I know the Dove would be my choice
to spread God's holy word

~~~~~~~~~~~~~~~~~~~~~~~~~~~
Valerie Peterson Brown
Jacksonville, Florida
~~~~~~~~~~~~~~~~~~~~~~~~~~~

The author, Valerie Peterson Brown resides in Florida USA, and is an active member of Allpoetry.com. She recently published her first Book "Devotions for the Wounded Warrior", and at present is working on three more. His faith and thanks for her gifts are given to God for it is through His favor that she has survived the adversities of life.

Our Lighthouse

There is One who watches
every move we make
One who gave so very much
to each and every one of us

There is no storm
that will ever bring us down
we're guided by the lighthouse
He stands there daily

With arms outstretched to us
He will catch us in His arms
there is no way we'll fall
as long as we will lean

On his outstretched arms
He is our wondrous savior
He is our closest friend
He is our only lighthouse

No matter what the storm
with arms outstretched
He'll guide us safely
into His open arms

The Person I Want To Be

There is inside of me a seed
of what my life could be
implanted is this simple creed
loving child of God, is my plea

Filled with faith given freely
by my Father from on high
knowing love ideally
never asking why

The gift of faith I now accept
it is my daily plea
all my strength is now adept
on this I will agree

I now can give all that I have
to be who He would have me be
my life with others to interweave
this is the golden key

To give myself to those in need
to be my Fathers child
to His wishes I concede
to know at me He smiles

Guide me now oh Lord I pray
rain on me with the love you give
from your love I'll never stray
transgressions you forgive

You my Lord are the message
let me daily sing your praise
You freed me from my bondage
daily I am amazed

You have given oh so much
to one lowly such as I
I'm guided by your loving touch
I will not wonder why

Be With Me Lord I Pray

Dear Lord this day I call to You
to hear me as I pray
abide with me each day
to guide me lest I stray
take my hand oh Lord I pray
reach out to those I love
protect them throughout their life
protect them from Satan's barbs

His horrifying attacks please stay
they belong to You oh Lord
their lives I place within Your hands
give them strength to face the day

Give them discernment to know the way
to travel safely in Your steps
to know You lead the way
their lives are in Your hands

Dear Lord protect each of my friends
their families and their friends
reach out to all those sick in sin
help them to ward off the attack
Lord You are my dearest friend
on You I can rely
be with me Lord in all I do
protect me lest I stray

My Prayer

Praise you oh Lord
Who lives on high
giving grace to all
caring to take the plunge
into your loving arms

Jesus Savior of my soul
Protector of my heart
guide to my feet that take
paths they should not trod

Jesus Savior of the world
guide the steps I take
give me strength to know
Your never failing will

I've come to a fork in my path
if I stay where I am is it
where I need to be
or should I take the chance
and step to take the other path

If I take the fork to
paths I have not trod
will that be in your precious
Will? guide me now, oh
precious Lord I pray

You know the road you've
planned for me
yet, here I stand confused
guide me Lord I pray
Make the steps that I must take
glow with holy light
let me follow in your steps
hold me in your loving arms this day
help me to know which is the right way

The Love of the Father

How do I tell of one great love
a love that's changed my life?
there is one love that reigns above
His love strikes down every strife

He's our Heavenly Father
He gave His son to save us
above Him there is no other
always He is with you

My life has never been the same
since He came into my ife
He rescued me from all my shame
and stands beside me in my grief

To live forever in His love
to daily give him praise
for He is as gentle as a dove
so simple are His ways

He's there for me through all my trials
He guides me when I'm lost
He looks at me and smiles
yes, He saved me, He paid the ultimate cost

A greater love could never be
than the Father's wondrous love
His love has set me free
no other stands above

Father to us all
His love will never fail
we can hold our heads high & stand tall
for His love will never fail

~~~~~~~~~~~~~~~~~~~~~~~~~~
Joyce Josephson
Reading, Massachusetts
~~~~~~~~~~~~~~~~~~~~~~~~~~

Joyce Josephson is a 52 year old woman who lives in New England. She is married and has one son, age sixteen. A graduate of Massachusetts College of Art and Design in 1984; she holds a BFA in Graphic Design

Joyce has been writing poetry and occasional song lyrics on a steady basis for the past four to five years. She is very active in her Christian community as a cantor, teacher and designer. She is also a freelance graphic designer, and has designed a line of inspirational greeting cards with her own verse, scripture verses and photographic images, many of which she has photographed and edited. She hopes to begin marketing them locally some time soon.

On Allpoetry, she designs borders and backgrounds as well as write poetry.

Joyce hopes that you enjoy her poetry, and that it gives glory to God.

Love

Love is patient
love is kind
bears fruitful branches
upon its vine

Love does not envy
it does not boast
love protects those
who need it most

Love is not proud
nor is it rude
love has a humble
attitude

Love does not anger
easily
love does not brood
over injury

Love does not rejoice
in doing wrong
love wants truth
to carry on

Love bears all things
through storm and gale
knowing love
will never fail

Hand of Grace

Grasp
my hands
please free me
from this quicksand

Mired in muck I'm plucked
from Satan's black bitter blame
mercifully cleansed of shame
thankful for your grace

Your abundant
promise of
Heaven's
gift
freely
given me
Eternal Life

On loving kindness
I rely knowing You own
a vast supply Your love shown
through sacred blood shed

Your rugged cross
paid the cost
soul freed
mine

The Cornerstone

He bore our cross, redeemed our home
freed us from death, robed us in white
Christ ransomed us; we are His own

His glory and dominion known
the Father's Son, His pure delight-
He bore our cross, redeemed our home

He left His glory and His throne
to cleanse us in God's holy sight
Christ ransomed us; we are His own

The Lamb of God cursed and alone
wore stench of sin to cure our plight
He bore our cross, redeemed our home

"Into your hands" His final moan
God's grace bestowed that day of night
Christ ransomed us; we are His own

On Easter Morn He moved the stone
our sins of stone crushed by Love's might
He bore our cross, redeemed our hom
Christ ransomed us; we are His own

His Peace Will Reign

hope
gives us
boldness to
dream vibrantly
translucent sparks of
painted light spray glitter
across summer night skies cast
borders framing children's visions
of sheep asleep beside the proud beast
God's peace will reign over heaven and earth

Feed the Need

Break with the hungry
my bountiful bread
with love beyond measure
my Lord Jesus said.
feed them with kindness
nourish their souls-
bread blest and broken
give it for free-
good food to sustain them
for their long journey

But where are the hungry
my dear Adonai?
they dwell all around you
He said in reply
he lonely, the hopeless
the broken, the worn-
they hunger for My love
they thirst for My peace
seat all at the table
and share My fine feast

When My children hunger
you are My feast
when My dear ones lose hope
you bring My peace
I build with your hands
I heal with your heart-
blest are the hungry
blest also are you
the mercy you give is
My mercy too

~~~~~~~~~~~~~~~~~~~~~~~~~~
Marianna Yemenitzi
Cyprus
~~~~~~~~~~~~~~~~~~~~~~~~~~

Marianna Yemenitzi, a South African Cypriot woman; lives in Cyprus and loves it. She's married to a Cypriot who was born in Cyprus, and came to South Africa at the age of five.
They have two wonderful sons and immigrated to Cyprus in 2000 to be closer to their families. She thinks it is really beautiful and wonderful to live on an island after living in a crime filled country. She loves the Lord above all else and He has been her comforter through many trials and tribulations.
She's always loved writing, and as a born-again Christian, the Lord is the center of her inspiration. Her love for the Lord gives her desire to share his word with all those she meets.
Her motto is:
The Lord is above all, for with Him nothing is impossible.

Glorious Love and Adoration

Glorious love and adoration
is spilling out of my soul
it is only you oh my Lord
that can make me feel so whole
I stand before you Lord
as your very humble servant
You oh Lord give in abundance
so that I should not want

Oh Lord how can I express
this deep, deep love I have inside
this love I have for you that
I really do not want to hide
I want to stand on the mountaintops
and of your love to shout!
To sing, praise and pray
and let my love for you pour out

I want to share this love I have
with everyone all around
that all that hear, what I have to say
will, with the same love abound
my heart is overflowing
filled with adoration for you
I want to share it with the whole
wide world so they will feel it too

Rejoice My Heart, My Soul, My Mind

Rejoice my heart, my soul, my mind
another day has dawned sublime
with love and grace and mercy true
this day to face with hope anew

Though some moments they do so grind
rejoice my heart, my soul, my mind
when another this day you meet
with smile and happiness do greet

The soul and will with purpose live
to mind and heart fulfilment give
rejoice my heart, my soul, my mind
do not let troubles make you blind

At the close of this wondrous day
bend your knee, to the Lord and pray
for He was faithful true and kind
rejoice my heart, my soul, my mind

God's Powerful Call

Standing at the top of the mountain, thinking I might fall
I hear in the distance God's powerful call
as I answer with a prayer, God's grace takes over my life
and all is still and calm, within there is no more strife
I look around and below, at the beauty all around, from here above
and know, that I have been showered, with His great love

The Redeeming Hand of God

In my despair I fell
not knowing which way to turn
I cried myself to sleep
gently, I felt His presence
the touch of His hand awoke me
the hand that brings
overwhelming
peace and comfort

The hand which is full of
support, provision
relief and strength
His tender touch
inexpressibly sweet
encouraged me to
rise

I came to the realization
that, if I was to ever be
raised up, it could only be
by the Hand of God
I fell prostrate before Him
in the knowledge that God
could do nothing for me until
I recognized my limitations
and allowed Him to do the
impossible

That Quiet Place Up High

Oh, how I long for that quiet place, up high
that place, where the only things moving
are the wind with my thoughts
communicating them to the Lord

Oh, for that quiet place, up high
where I can feel, the presence of His face
where I share in His love, feeling it
all over again, surrounding me

Oh for that quiet place, up there
where, I draw closer to God and
am totally refreshed and my strength
is renewed once more

In that very special place up high
where I feel His presence
His face, as I before him kneel
I offer Him, my life, and my all

~~~~~~~~~~~~~~~~~~~~~~~~~~~~~~~~
Melissa Sanders
Milton, Florida
~~~~~~~~~~~~~~~~~~~~~~~~~~~~~~~~

Melissa Sanders has been writing poetry for 7 years and believes this ability to spin words comes only from her Lord and Savior; Jesus Christ. It was after Salvation that she was able to write her first poem. She has raised her three children alone, with only God's help. She has been a Christian for 12 years. Most of her poetry is based on her personal relationship with God, with some focused on childhood abuse. All of her poetry is personal and very real.

In His Peace

Walking through this life scorned, mocked and jaded
by those who call themselves God's anointed
can at times get me down, weary and worn
but you see In His Peace - I am adorned

Trials and troubles at times over flow
arrows from Satan's evil, nasty bow
shot in wicked vengeance; swiftly arrive
but you see In His Peace - I am alive

False prophets come and go, quickly they fade
counting on their works, trusting what they made
pretentious, haughty, jealous and forlorn
but only In His Peace - I will adorn

In His Peace I have solid assurance
that I walk with Him; He's my endurance
found within His arms is the sweetest rest
and safely In His Peace - my soul will nest

I'll gladly give all to stay In His Peace
no self-righteous works, from them I will cease
my statement of Faith is contained herein
it's only In His Peace - I exist in

Passing All Understanding

Through Jesus comes God's perfect peace
our worries to Him we release
it passes all understanding
continually its expanding

By Jesus it's left as a gift
overcoming sins massive rift
between Holy God and mankind
His peace is a blessing to find

His peace is simply a knowing
with it life is easy going
it takes us through toil and trouble
unearths us from Satan's rubble

It's not found in earthly riches
but God's children it enriches
causing us to dwell thus secure
for God's peace is extremely pure

To the wicked there is no peace
no pardon nor sin's sweet release
simply unfulfilled desires
which draw them to hell's hot fires

Errant Faith

Errant faith is to put your trust
in other things; into works thrust
instead of just trusting in Him
count as enough God's Holy Gem

To errant faith I don't belong
because in the Lord I am strong
trusting ONLY in Jesus Christ
saved from Satan's attempted heist

In only Christ I dwell as safe
never wander, no more to waif
lead by His eye, no more to roam
for soon Heaven will be my home

Shadowed only by His dear hand
it is in Christ I understand
that He's enough, nothing besides
complete rescue in Him resides

I stand only in Jesus Christ
although Satan came to entice
washed in His blood, cleansed in His death
raised up anew, given new breath

There's only One way to be saved
only One name whereby sins waived
it's Jesus Christ, on Him believe
and Salvation, you will receive

Cleansing Rain

Washed in Cleansing Rain; refreshed and renewed
my dryness is quenched, my spirit pursued
by a Holy God, though sin was accrued

Amazing is He, my Rock, Redeemer
a shelter in storms, though I, a dreamer
a sure foundation, lover of my soul
I trust Him with me - I give Him control

He grasps who I am, He meets all my needs
understands my thoughts, yet His love exceeds
all limitations and things earthly known
cleansing Rain is found only at His throne

Let Me Be Found

Order Thy servant's steps Oh Lord
let me never fail Thee
guide me with Thy resplendent eyes
and never let me be

And when You call, my Father true
help me to answer yes
in faith I cleave only to Thee
may I never digress

Oh, Holy One, I seek Thy face
grant me sweet songs of peace
that overflow to those around
may that song not decrease

Pleasing to Thee, accepted firm
Father, let me be found
I abandon self, dreams and hope
let life by Thee be crowned

A spirit so poor and contrite
give I unto Thee Lord
fashion me now to Thy Own will
Thou art my sure reward

~~~~~~~~~~~~~~~~~~~~~~~~~
Carla Procida
West Islip, New York
~~~~~~~~~~~~~~~~~~~~~~~~~

Carla Procida is a 49 year old New Yorker, married to a Pastor for 29 years. Even though they have no children of their own, they have 10 children in India, for which they have built an orphanage. They also continually help needy children in the United States. Carla has had Parkinsons disease for over 10 years, but shows no outward symptoms, Her favorite quote is by the character played by Natalie Wood in Miracle on 34th St. "Faith is believing when common sense tells you not to".

All Our Dark Clouds

All my dark clouds
God's hands have wrung
found the lark's tongue
caused songs to be sung

A Friend That Sticks Close

There's a friend that sticks closer than a brother
since family can easily forget you, even a mother
and friends, though they are meant to last forever
we all know that even one disagreement can sever

So stick with One who will go through thick and thin
unconditionally love and forgive you when you sin
for when you were still dead in your transgressions
Jesus died so you could become His own possession

Please don't brush me off as some religious fanatic
or think I just want to cause fundamentalist static
I'm just someone who once walked in your shoes
and I'll go far as to ask, what do you have to lose?

Taking God's Word to the Heights

I gave Your Words not angels wings
to fly above the weighty things
nor that which keeps the eagles up
where icy peaks and clouds do sup
I took each promise for what I lack
and placed it on a sparrow's back
not because how high it flies
but Who would know where it lies

Drops Beautifying

Thank You Oh God
for shade from summer's sun
this tiny seed You grew up
which fought to crawl up
on the ripples of raindrops
coming down
from stormy skies above
breaking through dark soil
just to color the world
for a short season at best

Yet Your Son's lifetime
crowned in the final hours
love arose from bloody soil
drops beautifying
every child of Yours

So if I can bring joy
like Spring's first petals
clothed in Jesus
well then I know
my life has been worth it

A Perfect Side

I believe the most beautiful rainbow
stretches over the heart of God
colors converging at His throne
like diamonds set in purest gold

Shades of love through human eye
in streams of light dissolved
a tapestry of haphazard color
from Heaven, a panoramic view

From time's beginning to its end
God's masterpiece from higher view
trusting threads of trial and joy
through angel's eyes its perfect side

~~~~~~~~~~~~~~~~~~~~~~~~~
Bob Barra
Albuquerque, New Mexico
~~~~~~~~~~~~~~~~~~~~~~~~~

Bob Barra became interested in writing as a teenager through what he was reading then, which was mostly Science Fiction novels and short stories. Having great aspirations to be the next big science fiction author, at 18 he became burnt-out from all the writing. Then on July 3rd, 1992, he was saved by the Lord Jesus. A year thereafter, he found a great deal of material in the Bible, gaining the spiritual gift of encouragement; he began writing words of encouragement and eventually short Christian allegories.

He discovered journaling, chronicling his prayers and the answers he got. During that time, he discovered he would write poetic words of praise, much like the Psalms. Thereafter, he began pursuing poetry, which accounts for about 95% of what he writes now.

About Faith

Faith's indeed a divine gift
given from above
meant to heal a sin-borne rift
healed by His love

All have it; not just His own
all look for things believed
by it, His will could be known
or be kept deceived

Faith is finite, like a seed
as the Son had taught us
for this life, it's our need
to raise us from sin's dust

Paul had said, "Now abide"
with hope and love; those three
with these gifts, we can ride
the taunts and tests we see

Yet faith, like hope, is for "now"
for now is when we need them
after this life, out they bow
but Love's with us in heaven

The Highest Form

To touch the heart of God
having learned His will
to go to Him and prod
as we're being still

To seek His grace and mercy
in e'ery time and need
to see as He sees
it's for this, we plead

To Him, who knows all need
we dare not ask our way
the higher will is what we seek
when we seek to pray

Yet here is our greatest grace
prayer when it's most raw
is, once having seen His face
to fall before in awe

Plea

Sing the silent tune, and sing it very soon
we know not the end of season
be now very strong, for those who so stand long
will see His wisdom's reaso;

He's the only One, our God's begotten Son
as our Provision for the Way
by His death, He appeased; it's His blood that still pleas
"Come all, to Me, and pray"

Pray to the Son as Living Hope; seek His grace, for it grope
and end your war with God
for He made Him our Door, to find Life forever more
our sins He has forgot

Then, in Him, you will have peace; needed when Satan won't cease
especially when He owns you
His gift will be a heart so quiet, drowns out the world's ungodly riot
for you will see Him true

And by that Truth you'll come to see, beyond all proof you will be free
to cross the threshold of death
for by the Key of your salvation, death becomes your graduation;
He holds His children's breath

Eternal Joy

Last breath on earth is breathed in pain
followed by first praising His name
living Water brought me here
to the One I'm always near
trials have ended; Joy's Day has come
old afflictions seem light b'fore the Son
my strength returns; for grief has died
I stand before Him, my sole Abide
love erases my history of sin
the Love by which I'm borne again
and all the saints surround me so
elating fellowship that sparks a glow
I'm so glad that me He's won
seeing my life's barely begun

Power of Three

There is beauty in prayer
with a brother
seeking Your strength
You are delighted
as we fight together
against that which is contrary
to Your desire

When we see one of our own
weakened by the fiery darts
of the evil one, it is Your pleasure
that we stand with them
Your grace of prayer
given to us, is a mighty weapon
all we need do is stand together
to Your glory, for that which endures

We can stand against spiritual contradictions
the world, the enemy and our fleshly minds
thus, by Your Spirit
we step closer to the image
You alone have prepared for us
greater than this
we continue in glorious fellowship
with You

The enemy flees
in frustration and defeat
the victory is ours
the glory, with Your pleasure
is solely Yours

Praise the Lord for the three-fold cord

~~~~~~~~~~~~~~~~~~~~~~~~~
Debi Kinch
Gladwin, Michigan
~~~~~~~~~~~~~~~~~~~~~~~~~

Living in the heart of north central lower Michigan, Debi Kinch enjoys small town life with her husband, David. When not at her computer reading or writing poetry or designing backgrounds, she enjoys birdwatching, and reading her bible and time spent with her children and grandchildren.

Free To Whoever Wants

Bought and paid for
by His Blood

I have a Savior
His name is Jesus
He's free

He wants a new home
in your heart

The handle to your heart
lies inside of you
He's free

Only you can open the door
invite Him in

You will be glad you did
the benefits are amazing
He's free

The retirement plan is awesome
a heavenly package for you

Thank You

As the sun sets on this day
casting a lingering ray
across the mid summer sky
cannot help but question why

Why your blessings come to me
fFound a sinner, yet set free
thank you dear Lord for this gift
giving my soul such a lift

In your sunset I can see
all the love you have for me

In You

My God
you are so wonderful

In you
I am secure

No matter what happens
I am not afraid

For with me you are
everything that's dear
though rocks and stones are harmful
no matter what man does

Thoughts of eternity
will see me through

Nowhere To Hide

I stand before the mirror
looking to see behind me
no matter which way I turn
I cannot see there
for I block my own view
a place where sins do hide
but ...
when I stand before Jesus
myself will no longer block my way
I will be able to see before
and all around, including behind
there will be no where to hide
for all will be seen

My King

Death
Jesus died
just for you and me
He rose just to set us free
love

~~~~~~~~~~~~~~~~~~~~~~~~~~~
Vickie Mosely
Midland, Texas
~~~~~~~~~~~~~~~~~~~~~~~~~~~

Vickie Mosely wears numerous "hats". She is a wife, mother, grandmother, teacher, poet, artist and last but not least prayer warrior.

After teaching for 17 years, she has returned to school to become a nurse with the goal of becoming a medical missionary. Her poetry delves into the human experience of conflicts, emotions and challenges that she as well as all of us face. Her own experiences of life make it possible for her poems to relate to us all.

God Places Value

Value, something most of us desire to possess
for others to look upon and deem us worthy of value
often measured by how great is our success
are we worthy of the value that has been assigned us?

However, there is One who has considered our value
we were wanting and came up lacking
our value fell short, but He paid the dues
He deemed us worthy through the death of His Son

Accepting His garment to cover our sins
God regards us as a value to His Kingdom
He offers us a chance to once again begin
trade our hell bound lives into those that hold value

False Witness

Trustworthiness-an honorable thing to aspire to
but something few choose to do

God placed importance on this very attribute
as one of His ten commandments, He did commute

His nineth rule "Thou shalt not bear false witness"
as with the other nine, remains timeless

Some may tag it as the "credibility gap" or
"a white lie", but it is something God still abhors

It's one of God's commandments just the same
one of the ten Abraham proclaimed

In short it's a lie, falls far short of the truth
told to cause harm and He considers it quite uncouth

Especially since God has told us to love one another
and to discredit someone's character unfairly is lacking in candor

Unknowingly we teach our children early to lie
and when they are caught, we wonder why

Speaking untruths about our neighbor in God's book is taboo
He is displeased when the facts, by us, are misconstrued

So let us not forget-all the commandments should be obeyed
and on not one should we sway

Promise

Promise
was given us
with a firm assurance
the Holy Spirit would soon come
to comfort the believers left behind
to help us with intercession
groanings not understood
by any man
promise

Have I thanked You

Dear Heavenly Father
have I stopped to tell you
that I love you today?

Have I even mentioned
how grateful I am to say
that I belong to you
because of the price your Son has paid?

Thank you for the many
answered prayers I saw this day

Thank you for always being
available, with open hands extended my way
for being mindful of your children
and loving us even when we disobey

Thank you that you made a way
for us to be with you eternally
a place reserved for us in Heaven
when we have finished our journey
and the day that has been appointed
has arrived very timely

Remaking Me

I started this journey
that I needed to make
asking God
to do what it takes
I wanted to be mended
and molded by Him
He had a lot of work to do
before we could begin

Broken and crushed down to my soul
I was willing to do what I was told
walls were put up, that had to come down
He told me "learn to forgive
in order to live"

Feeling exposed with nowhere to hide
emotions were running rampant inside

Feelings of anger, hurt and hate
held me in bondage to this very date
these had to be replaced with forgiveness and love
fruits that only come from above

I am a work that will never be finished
I want to be molded and crafted daily
in the image of Him
for that's where my new life really begins

~~~~~~~~~~~~~~~~~~~~~~~~~~~~~~
Diane L. Busch
Sandy, Utah
~~~~~~~~~~~~~~~~~~~~~~~~~~~~~~

Diane L. Busch is the first of six children, and grew up in the beautiful Bitterroot Valley of Montana, and the Bay Area of California. The Lord has been ever kind and patient, strengthening and teaching her in her trials and struggles.

My Hurt

My rainbow bruise and abraded knee
I parade in lament before Him
tutoring Him as to my suffering
He tenderly wipes my tears
whose trickling I trace into wounded palm
speechless, I fall to discover penetrated feet
am gently enfolded in His embrace
His eyes lovingly withholding
His knowledge of paths of pain
anguish of soul I cannot comprehend

Lord

Ye who are my guardian
gate, sure path and prize
with unuttered beauty
lift to Thee mine eyes

Teach me in my trials
comfort, all to bear
that I may stand a certain witness
of Thy tender care

Trumpet rising glory
with the eastern sky
wake the world to gladness
dry night's tears we cry

Unfurl the majesty of grace
with Thy wound-pierced hand
each repentant claims Thy love-wing
willing chicks of man

Graven Upon the Palms of His Hands

He who numbers each sand of the shore
knows my every hourglass grain
Who fashioned the spiralling galaxies
shaped my small life's domain

Who spies the secret fox's hole
sees all my silent pain
fingers that lit bright heaven's stars
will wipe from my cheeks grief's rain

He calls, He knocks, He stands and waits
eternity's perfect guest
with quiet gifts of charity
cleansing, peace and rest

'til self-sufficiency's party noise
my roaring, burning pride
leave me cold and alone in the ashes
and I hear, and invite Him inside

Why such bother? My hands are so dirty
my heart's been so often beguiled
my soul finds itself clothed in tatters
yet He reaches, and calls me His child

Praise

Who can say enough good about God?
and how shall my poor lips praise Him?
He hath brought me forth from a hard place
and made my portion among the blessed
daily I drink from pure waters of loving-kindness
poured upon my thirsting soul by His infinite goodness
and the tender compassion of mine own into whose arms I am fallen
I hunger not, and am filled with milk and honey
Manna moments cover my daily walk
sweet bounty of His compassion without measure
filling every aching famine for hands willing
to gather His constantly renewed, ever satisfying gifts

Weak Things

O God

Thou hast lifted these hands
that hang down with weariness
and filled them with good gifts
even with strength in the vital hour
when my basket was empty
but for Thy graciousness

Thou hast strengthened my feeble knees to
join step with another's tired tread
whispered the secrets of fierce hearts
and enlarged my understanding
Thou hast taught me compassion because I was willing
and turned not away back
from seeking the paths of Thy righteousness

Thou hast prolonged my days upon the earth
upon the paths of the living have I continued
my children have not lamented in the shadow
with the motherless, nor known the sorrow of
anchorless grief in the absence of the distaff
to rise as doves to daybreak, ever mourning

All this Thou hast done, because I asked it Thee
and it was not contrary to Thy purpose
O God, my surety in all my days
my peace, cradle and support

art Thou

~~~~~~~~~~~~~~~~~~~~~~~~~~
Pamela Mae Rhew Bush
Mascoutah, Illinois
~~~~~~~~~~~~~~~~~~~~~~~~~~

Pamela Mae Rhew Bush is a born again Christian and founder of a prayer group at Allpoetry.com. She loves the Lord, and it was that love which prompted her to write her first book, "He Is Worthy: Poetic Words of Praise and Worship". Since then she has published a book on her own, "Glorifying His Name" and has had several pieces published in different books, both prior and since her first book.

A loving wife, mother of two and grand-mother; she continues daily to stay in the will of God, and share the Love of Christ in her poetry.

Happiness Overflows

Having true joy within my soul
A gift the Lord has given me
Praising Him throughout my day
Praying I'll walk in His will
I'm not always filled with happiness
Nothing can steal my spiritual joy
Every sunrise I am blessed to see
Shines brightly, and warms my heart
Son of God, thank you for your love

On the cross you took all mans sin away
Vowing forgiveness to us with your blood
Emitting blessings from the beginning
Rendering to us a chance at life
Father in Heaven sent you to us
Loving us mercifully, and with grace
Our choices we make everyday
Will decide if we get life or death
Serving you Lord, is the choice I made

My Father

My love for God overflows
Yahweh shed His blood, taking the blame

Father who has blessed me so
Allow me now to praise your name
To you my heart I do bestow
Hear me Lord, forgive my shame
Every day you let me know
Repented sins I need not claim

You Hold My Happiness

I seek to do your will Lord
for meaning in my life
all else is simply meaningless
and fills my soul with strife

You alone hold my happiness
my joy you gave to me
covered by your blood Lord
forever I am free

Each day you bestow blessings
though undeserving as I am
it is by your righteousness
I've been accepted as your lamb

Thank you for your mercy
please show me in your word
what you have planned for me
let your still small voice be heard

Always There

Almighty God
how does one praise One so awe-inspiring?
Your loving and forgiving heart
allows us to call you Father

We need only call upon You
in the name of Your Son
Jesus
their is none other

Your Spirit dwells within us
when we call upon Your mercy
seeking forgiveness
we receive Your grace

Do we then humble ourselves
and walk always in Your will?
of course not
we fall on our face

Then You lift us up
consolingly
exonerative
replete with love

Never do You forsake us
even when we leave You behind
You're always there
watching from above

I Thank You God

You hear our prayers
knowing what's best
from a Heart that cares
our lives are blest

If the answer's no
it's for our own good
you're omniscient
oft times misunderstood

I thank you God
in Jesus name
your supremeness
I proudly proclaim

Frank Hanson
Homedale, Idaho

Frank Hanson is a 49 year old happily married man who loves the Lord with all his heart. His life has seen many bumps and turns, and he didn't always know the truth of Jesus Christ. He, like many of his brothers and sisters, learned of the Lord through His mercy and calling. Never to be the same again, and no matter how many times he falls, Frank knows there is no turning back on the One who sacrificed all for him and has promised eternity worshipping His name, which he will do, so ever humbly and gratefully.

True Balance

There are choices we make to fill our needs
to feed the desires until our soul bleeds
we pick and choose what's harmful and unclean
as we unbalance the scale of our inner being

When the flesh chooses what the soul abhors
we justify our decisions by closing the minds door
raise the desire and push down what is right
we corrupt the spirit until it's out of sight

We figure we'll make choices for ourselves now
and later make up for it someway, somehow
a good deed here and a kind word there
we ease our conscience out of utter despair

As we seek to balance this fragile scale
with unselfish acts through a clouded veil
we must stop and think about our motives indeed
for unless they are pure, we will never succeed

When we act out of guilt to ease our mind
can we hide our motives from the Lord Divine?
If we could only see how we are seen
would we be ashamed of our mortal being?

What will happen to our human condition
if we lose the will to change our position?
when the scales have tipped out of proportion
we lose the ability to see through the distortion

We are but finite beings of flesh and bone
with no way to win this battle on our own
we are but lambs that await destruction
by the world, flesh and devils instruction

But fear not my friends, for hope is not lost
if you turn to the One who died on the cross
it is by His name, His blood and His love story
that your eternal scale will be balanced in glory

My Prayer

Oh Dear Lord, grant me your time
as I bend these knees before thy throne Divine
gather my prayers, blessed Spirit on high
these babblings, this confusion from thy child's mind

Please take these grumblings and imperfect thoughts
clean them with thy truth, Holy Spirit of God
for you are the One who can truly see
into the heart of this sinner, into my deepest need

Today I come to you, My Lord, My God with no special
Request
not world hunger, not world peace, no one to bless
for these things I know are all in your sight
blessed God of creation, maker of light

With so much pain in this world I see
I petition a moment of precious time with me
the need I have is simple and true
a flicker, a glance, one of those rare moments with you

In this life of highs and lows
the greatest moments are the ones you've chose
fleeting memories in time, gone too fast
where a glimpse of true love, barely lasts

All the riches on earth can not compete
to one brief moment at thy feet
for when I'm in your presence my Lord, my God
love's true meaning flows down from heaven above

So, if it be your will my Savior, my God
I'd ask for one moment of communion in love
but if this moment that I long to feel
is for another time, I bow to thy will

For I know this true, so clear in my mind
that it's you my Lord, that has reserved the time
to fill my soul to renew my spirit
oh, precious gift, how I long to be near it

So, Lord as I declare my groanings to you
brought by the Holy Spirit and in the name of Jesus too
I ask for your strength as I wait upon your call
to meet again in that moment where love surpasses all

AMEN

I Will Follow

Lord, I take up my cross to follow you
battling the world, flesh and the devil too
to follow you fully, is my hearts desire
death to a life that only leads to the fire

Ashamed, I am not and never ever shall be
of you my Lord, my only God, my only King
with eyes wide open by the Holy Spirit's hand
it's your light I will seek in this mortal land

Once these thoughts were so strange to me
suffering and dieing for something unseen
I now chuckle and laugh about a man so blind
I would die for you my precious Lord, anytime

Oh how I know, I'm not perfect in so many ways
with failures that eat away at my numbered days
there's one thing alone, I know with all that I am
you are my God and I am forever your humble lamb

Lord, Who Will I Be

Dear Lord, I thank you for my life on earth
you have showed me many things, since my rebirth
My eyes have been opened to your wondrous creation
with joyous new sight of my eternal salvation

Your mercy is far beyond my understanding
to love a worm as I is truly dumbfounding
With mistakes and detours that I often take
Lord what am I, but a constant heartache

I think about this life so consumed with sin
the greed, the lust, this human nature within
And to make it even worse, my Lord Divine
I justify my sins against the scale of my kind

With this war that rages on from the old man to the new
I am formed and molded by the world, flesh and devil too
With the Holy Spirit awakening my soul
the battle for who I am becomes four fold

I know that my salvation is firmly intact
with the death of my Savior 2000 years back
But my mind keeps pondering and I cannot see
that when I reach my eternal home, who will I be?

From a man without knowledge, I know this is true
In humility and meekness, I ask this of you
When you take away all that I see is me
what will be left in heaven to worship thee?

When I reunite with family and friends
will they know me and I them?
Will we embrace and laugh as in the mortal coil
when most of who we were, was of earthly spoils

I know not what will be left of me
but there's a yearning, a longing for my greater being
I worship and praise you my glorious Lord
as I wait my transition at heavens door

A Moment With The Lord

by Frank Hanson

I kneel before you Lord in this humble earthly shell
and again ask forgiveness of things only you, I can tell

Things I have brought before you, so many times before
cries from a broken soul that forever knocks at your door

This pain from new eyes that have been opened to the truth
such a gift, such a curse, to see what is unclean and uncouth

It hurts my soul so much when the old self always reappears
Oh Lord! I have battled so hard through an ocean of tears

But, through this glass darkly, you have not left me alone
for there is a grain of vision, about a place I'll soon call home

Where your glory and wonder awaits beyond this short night
A place where tears are devoured by your loves perfect light

I must hold to your words given at the moment of rebirth
A gentle message of love about this worm of eternal worth

It is in that message you have always whispered in my ear
where I've found strength to sustain me through the years

So, I shall repeat this mortal dance from the old to the new
and endure the heartaches of a nature that sins against you

As I awaken each new day, I plead for thy true guiding light
You are forever my safe haven, through the darkest of nights

AMEN

Alter Call

God is always there for us, waiting patiently for us to draw nigh to His call. He sent His Son Jesus Christ to cover our sins with His Blood, so that we may have peace and be set free. We need only confess our sins, and profess that Jesus is our Savior, accepting Him into our hearts. What a glorious day it is, when we give our lives to the Lord. We never need walk in fear again.

Pamela Mae Rhew Bush

www.ingramcontent.com/pod-product-compliance
Lightning Source LLC
Chambersburg PA
CBHW032134040426
42449CB00005B/243